Foreword

It gives me immense pleasure to write a few words about this book which is specially designed to test listening comprehension of learners at the tertiary level. The most unique thing about the book is that material used is in Indian context.

In addition this, the things cover different dimensions such as education, general awareness and Inspirational ones. There are also couple of interviews and passages that would have an appeal to the learners especially their sense of humour and also inculcate in them certain values. The author is indebted to the Youtube from where this material has been procured. In learning language listening is one of the significant receptive skills that inspires young learners to listen meaningfully and speak whenever they are offered an opportunity. It is heartening to note that most of the material caries Indian context and British accent. Though it does not include the American variety, it would be useful to the learners and expose them to a wide variety of listening materials which are followed by though provoking MCQs and short answer questions. The transcriptions of the material have been incorporated in the text.

I hope such an endeavor will go a long way in consolidating listening skills.

Dr. Piyush Joshi

15/05/2015

Why was this book written?

It was written to help in testing the listening skills at tertiary level. The tasks will help not only to test the memory but understanding and interpretation of the learners. In addition to that this book also can be used to practice listening as the transcription is provided. So this book can be used in classroom by teachers or students can use it for their self-study.

Table of contents

Foreword
Using this book
1. Activity 1 — 1
    a) Transcription
    b) Task
2. Activity 2 — 8
    a) Transcription
    b) Task
3. Activity 3 — 13
    a) Transcription
    b) Task
4. Activity 4 — 17
    a) Transcription
    b) Task
5. Activity 5 — 21
    a) Transcription
    b) Task
6. Activity 6 — 25
    a) Transcription
    b) Task
7. Activity 7 — 32
    a) Transcription
    b) Task
8. Activity 8 — 37
    a) Transcription
    b) Task
9. Activity 9 — 43
    a) Transcription
    b) Task
10. Activity 10 — 51
    a) Transcription
    b) Task
References — 63

TRANSCRIPTION 1
A MOM AT THE SCHOOL

Saturday will go, Sunday will go and Monday will come and you will go back to the class and like this the teacher by name Mrs. Thomson entered the class for the first time and she had this habit of starting her class by saying 'love you all'. But she knew, she was lying because she could not feel that love for one of the students in the class who was very unkept, untidy and there was nothing in the child that drew attention from Mrs. Thomson. She was little indifferent to the child. She picked him for every negative example and ignored him for all the positive reasons. That year she has written the progress report for the first quarter and it was a system in the school that the headmaster has to counter sign every progress report. The administrators call for Mrs. Thomson and told Mrs. Thomson a progress report should report some progress. It should make a parent feel my child has a future. The way you have written the progress report for Teddy, that is how he was called. The way you have written progress report for Teddy, parents will give upon Teddy. Mrs. Thomson immediately said there is nothing I can do; I have nothing positive to write about the child. Immediately the headmaster asked the administer staff of the school to trace the old year's progress report of Teddy and sent it across to Mrs. Thomson's class. Mrs. Thomson saw the third standard progress report and it was written the final remarks 'the Teddy it the brightest child in the class.' She was stunned by what she read. She saw the fourth standard progress report and progressively all the remarks suggested, the teddy's mother was suffering from terminal cancer. She is not able to give the attention she used to give to the Teddy and it's just beginning to show up on the performance of Teddy. The first standard progress report read, Teddy has lost his mother and along with that himself. He desperately needs help otherwise we will lose this child. By then there were tears in the eyes of Mrs. Thomson, she looked at the principal and said I know what to do and she went back to the class. Probably it was a Monday morning. She walked into the class and again from the dyes of the class, looked at the class and said 'love you all' but she knew she was lying. The love she was feeling for Teddy right now was far far greater than the rest of the class. She decided that she is going to change her approach, for every positive reason Teddy's name was called. There was no more a negative reference to the whole thing. The last day of the school came, all the children had brought some gifts for the teacher, there was only one gift which was wrapped up in an old news paper. Somehow the sense of the teacher, she could new that it must be from Teddy. She opened that first a half used perfume bottle and a bracelet from which a few stones had already fallen was there. The whole class laughed knowing it was from Teddy. But without saying anything Mrs. Thomson just took that half used perfume bottle, sprayed it on her, wore that bracelet with a quarter smile. It seems, Teddy told now you are smelling like my mother. This is the last perfume that she used before she left me and this what was removed from her body before she was taken into the coffin. One year later, end of the school, end of the year, there was a letter on the Mrs. Thomson's table 'I have seen few more teachers but you are still the best teacher I have ever seen. With love, Teddy.' Every year till the end of the year Mrs. Thomson used to get this letter from the Teddy, 'I have seen few more teachers but you are the best teacher I have ever seen. With love, Teddy.' Years roll by they lost contact. Somewhere an agent traced Mrs. Thomson who had retired by now, and handed over a letter and the letter was signed 'Dr. Theodor, Ph.D.' Teddy had gone on to become a Ph.D. and the letter read, 'I have seen many more people in life Mrs. Thomson, this is your Teddy you are still the best teacher I have ever seen. I am getting married and I cannot dream of getting married without your presence along with that enclosed were to and fro flight tickets. Mrs. Thomson could not resist, she no more hand the perfume bottle but she still preserved the bracelet, she wore that and went to the church. She was trying to sit in the last row but volunteers identified and assured her right to the front row. And right to the front row there was a seat with the placard written 'mother'. Theodor personally asked Mrs. Thomson to sit in the chair and whisper 'you are the closest to my mother's that I have ever experienced and whatever i am today it's because of you mam. The wedding happened and after the wedding Theodor introduce Mrs. Thomson to his newly wedded wife, 'without her I wouldn't be where I am today.' There were tears in Theodor's eyes. It sees, Mrs. Thomson told the newly wedded woman 'without Teddy I would have never realised, the teacher must first be a mother to the every student of hers and only then a teacher.'

This is just my request to all of you, there is a teddy sitting in your class when you go back to yours classroom on Monday morning there is a Teddy in the class and you can be that Mrs. Thomson, please on Monday don't go back to the institute as a teacher, go back as a parent who can also be a teacher and be a turning point in the life of those children. You plus me, I believe we can build a new world.

TASK 1

Listen to the video/audio carefully and choose the most appropriate answer for the following questions.

1. **Why did the speaker say that the teacher, Mrs. Thomson, was indifferent to the child?**

   A) Because she stated child's name for every negative examples.

   B) Because the child was unkempt and untidy.

   C) Because the child was poor in studies and therefore she could not feel love for him.

   D) Because she ignored the child for good and stated for negative examples.

2. **"The way you have written the progress report for Teddy, parents will give up on Teddy."—What does the speaker mean by underlined word in above mentioned sentence?**

   A) They will be upset, will not think about his future and throw their hands up.

   B) They will stop dreaming for his future and accept that he cannot study.

   C) They will withdraw him from the school and will think of something else for him.

   D) They will encourage him and help him about the future and motivate him to give more attention to study.

3. **What was Mrs. Thomson's reaction when she watched Teddy's 3rd standard progress report?**

       A) She was confused   C) She was amused

       B) She was shocked   D) She was upset

4. Second time when Mrs. Thomson started her class by saying 'love you all' she was indifferent to _____.
   A) Teddy   C) Class
   B) Teddy's mother   D) The other guy

5. What was there in the gift wrapped up in the old news paper?
   A) A half used perfume bottle and necklace
   B) A perfume bottle and necklace
   C) A half used perfume bottle and a bracelet
   D) A Juice bottle and bracelet

6. After having discussion with the principal the teacher changed her_____ to the child.
   A) Thinking   C) Perspective
   B) Feeling   D) Liking

Read the questions carefully and write down appropriate answer.

1. What does Teddy mean when he said "now you are smelling like my mother."

   _____
   _____
   _____
   _____
   _____

2. What is the speaker's message through the speech? Write in your words.

   _____
   _____
   _____
   _____
   _____

TRANSCRIPTION 2
A TRUTH ABOUT BEING HAPPY

Sadguru	:	On a certain day Shankar Pillai went to the bar to drink with his friends. He just thought he will have just one shot and go home. But you know once they have a little bit of drink they become timeless like Yogis. So a few drinks happened then he looked at the watch like this, it was 2 a.m. but the wife's rule at the home is 8 p.m. he must be home and its 2 a.m. He got really disturbed and he wanted to rush back home so he thought he will find a shortcut and started running through somebody's garden and because of unknown terrain and also....
Anupam Kher	:	Drunk
Sadguru	:	....all the things inside, he flipped over and fell in to a rose bush face-down, all got scratched up, somehow found way to the house, it took him another 20 minutes to find the keyhole. He has found that and just slowly crawled up and went into the bathroom and looked at himself he looked true mess. So he opened medicine cabinet and wiped himself,

took band-aid, fixed himself then slowly crawled into the bed and slept. Morning 8 o'clock the wife brought a bucket full of cold water threw it on him and asked him to wake up. He got up.

She said, "You fool once again drinking?"

He said, "No honey since I promised you six months ago I haven't touched a drop."

She held him by the shirt, dragged him into the bathroom and showed him, all the band-aids were on the mirror.

TASK 2

Listen to the audio/video carefully and choose the most appropriate answer for the following questions.

1. Once people have little bit of drink they become _____ like yogis.

   A) Timeless
   B) B) time bound
   C) C) senseless
   D) D) meaningless

2. What was the wife's rule for husband to reach the home?

   A) Husband should reach home before 2 a.m.
   B) Husband should reach home before 8 a.m.
   C) Husband should reach home before 8 p.m.
   D) Husband should reach home before 1 a.m.

3. Sankaran Pillai flipped over and fell into a _____ due to all the things inside and unknown _____

   A) rose bush, Terrain
   B) rose bush, Garden
   C) rose bush, Road
   D) rose bush, Short cut

4. What did Sankaran's wife do to wake him up?

   A) Threw him off the bed
   B) Threw a bucket full of cold water
   C) Threw a bucket full of water
   D) Dragged him by holding his collar

5. Sankaran Pillai promised his wife _____ months ago.

   A) Six   B) sixty   C) sixteen   D) five

6. She _____ him by the shirt _____ him to the bathroom.

   A) Picked, dragged   C) held, dragged
   B) Snatched, pulled   D) held, ushered

7. What was pasted on the bathroom mirror?

   A) Band aids   C) wine
   B) Scratches   D) dirt

Read the questions carefully and write down appropriate answer.

8. Sankaran Pillai took 20 minutes to find out key hole because_____

   _____
   _____
   _____
   _____
   _____

9. What does the speaker mean by the word 'flipped over'?

   _____
   _____
   _____

10. Recall the punch line of the talk that makes the talk humorous?

_____

_____

_____

_____

TRANSCRIPTION 3
LAUGHTER IN FAMILIES

Laughter is no more part of family. My grandmother generation when they used to laugh they used to roll on the floor and laugh. I am sure some of you have seen your grandmothers or some of your mothers still do that, rocking laughter, they will roll on the floor and laugh, the whole body will vibrate at laughter, tears will come out of laughter, then that generation went then this generation has come where you need laughing club, where you go in the morning and there is the leadership for the laughing who tells to you 'go' and then all of you go 'ha..ha..ha..' looks like circus. It doesn't look like laughter. But you are a ok generation at least. The next generation is the kerchief generation.

'hmmm.. hmmmm' , 'excuse me'. And it's going to be worse the next generation whenever there is an occasion to laugh they will tell you 'LOL', 'L...O...L...' then you have to understand you have to laugh out loud, they won't even laugh it'll all to be communicated or one smiley will be sent to you. So is it any wonder we need so much psychologist and psychiatrist to deal with day-to-day issues. Laughter has to come back to the families. See if we don't learn to see the lighter side of life, and lighter side of life is most beautiful aspect of life.

You get upset about everything. You call somebody on the phone and somebody is not picking up and you should be able to laugh at it. And from here you get stick 'pick up...pick up...' whom are you telling?

Whom are you telling ?

You get angry at a soap that slips out of your hand in the bathroom *'samiya'*

Is it? to the soap?

That means your reflections are becoming weak and you have to do something about it. laughter has to come back to families.

TASK 3

Listen to the audio/video carefully and choose the most appropriate answer for the following questions.

1. What does the speaker say about the current generation with regards to laughter? They need _____
   - A) funny incidents
   - B) laughing Guru
   - C) laughing club
   - D) laughing friends

2. The speaker labels the next generation as _____ generation.
   - A) Kerchief
   - B) sophisticated
   - C) shy
   - D) courteous

3. The acronym LOL stands for _____
   - A) Laugh out loudly
   - C) laugh out loud
   - B) Lots of laugh
   - D) laugh out louder

4. According to the speaker laughter is associated with _____
   - A) Lighter side of life
   - C) ironical side of life
   - B) Grave side of life
   - D) ridiculous side of life

5. According to the speaker a man gets angry even at a/an _____ matter such as a cake of soap slipping out of hand in bathroom.
   - A) Humorous
   - B) insignificant
   - C) significant
   - D) natural

Read the questions carefully and write down appropriate answer.

6. Recall two significant characteristics that the speaker mentions about laughing style of grandmother's generation.

_____
_____
_____
_____

7. Why, do you think, the speaker compares laughing club with circus?

_____
_____
_____

8. Why does the modern man, according to the speaker require the help of psychologists and psychiatrists?

_____
_____
_____
_____

TRANSCRIPTION 4
HOW THE INTERNET IS CHANGING LANGUAGE

Technology always changes a language when printing came in the fourteen hundreds it changed the language, new styles developed, new spellings, new punctuation systems and so on. When the telephone came in the nineteenth century it changed the language, new patterns of dialogue came into being. When broadcasting started in the nineteen twenties it changed the language. Think about styles in the broadcasting medium that we didn't have before like sports commentaries and news reading and weather forecasting and chat shows and all of that and when the internet came into being it changed the language but nobody I think ever expected the language to be so diversified. As a result of the internet simply because nobody was able to predict exactly how many different technological variation of going to be of electronically mediated communication. I mean just think there is a world wide web, there is email, there is chat rooms. There is the virtual world the dungeons and dragons games people play. There is blogging, there is instant messaging, there is social networking sites now like youtube and facebook, there is twittering, there is mobile phone texting and it goes on and on and on. Now each one of these new technologies or new opportunities for communication produces a new kind of language. In the case of English, a new style of English, the language we use for web blogging is not the same as the language we use in instant messaging and so on we can gone through all these different mediums and point to new styles of English that a emerging as a consequence. The actual language itself hasn't changed that much. It is in the case that as you look through these different technological manifestations of English you see new grammar for instance. We don't get new patterns of grammar emerging, new types of verb ending or anything like that, nor is that much new vocabulary actually, adding a few hundred new words have come into English as a consequence of the internet but that's not very many considering the more than a million words that there are in English. New pronunciations not really! New punctuations, yes a bit, that you do certainly get new features of punctuation arriving on the internet emoticon for example being used in cleaver ways. People using punctuation in an exaggerated form that they never used to do before simply because you can hold the keys down, people can say fantastic, exclamation mark, exclamation mark, exclamation mark, and you can go on and on and on, for as long as you like. So there are a few novelty features like that but on the whole you look at the screen at what you see on the screen is the same kind of English language that you saw before the internet came into existence except now that these new styles to exploit the language has become expressively richer as a result of the internet.

TASK 4

Listen to the audio/video carefully and choose the most appropriate answer for the following questions.

1. **What came in 1400s that changed the English language?**

    A) Printing   B) orality   C) writing   D) rhetoric

2. **The 1400 brought about a change in the language in areas of_____**

    A) Style, spelling and punctuation

    B) Sentence pattern, style

    C) Punctuation, spelling, jargons

    D) Development in vocabulary, spelling and punctuation

3. **_____ came in the 19th century, it changed the language and gave New patterns of dialogues**

    A) Telephone   C) printing

    B) Radio   D) news paper

4. **In 1920s _____ came in to existence used for sports commentary, news reading, weather forecasting and chat shows.**

    A) Broadcasting   B) Radio   C) TV   D) Telephone

5. **Which social networking sites David Crystal mentioned in his talk?**
   A) Facebook, youtube and tweeter
   B) Facebook and tweeter
   C) Blog, wiki and facebook
   D) Hi5, facebook, tweeter

6. **All these technologies or new opportunities for communications produce a new kind of _____.**
   A) Discourse   B) language   C) Register   D) lingua

7. **The speaker says that people use punctuation mark in _____ way.**
   A) Frequent   B) exaggerated   C) normal   D) usual

8. **The speaker says that the inventions in technology have _____ actual language.**
   A) Changed   B) made richer   C) modified   D) ruined

TRANSCRIPTION 5
HOW TO DEAL WITH ANGER

Something really beautiful to learn about anger is this, when you go for a walk, in many houses dogs are there, that side of the gate I am talking. Ok... haha... And you don't have to do anything, from wherever you are you have to simply look at the dog and say 'ssshhhaaaa....' immediately it will start barking. Almost unless it's been completely trained 90 per cent of the dogs can be provoked. You don't have to do anything. It had enough for him. That's why it called an animal. The point I am asking here is if anybody can provoke you into becoming angry, anybody in the world has to only look at you and do like that.. *'yannnaa yannaa ppoo.'* Look at the question I am not asking who are you, I am asking who are you. That's all. If anybody in the world can provoke you to react, what are you? Anger is your weakness it has nothing to do with the world. Being through the whole thing its hit, reducing anger drop it. And it comes out of you wanting to be the master of the situation, in anger you are the victim of the situation. I just want you to understand, I am not telling you everybody is a "Vigneswari' and today you will be able to drop. But I want you to understand, you are losing control of the situation that's why you are getting angry. You don't feel like the master of the situation, you are getting provoked. And when you feel you are not in control of the situation when nothing works you feel this will work. So more and more you ask yourself, do I want to be the master of the situation or do I want to be a slave of the circumstances. Just keep asking question yourself this question. Even if anger doesn't go away let's take the first step, let's stop justifying your anger. Because the damage by your anger to you is far greater than to the entire world. Because when you are angry acids get secreted in your system and acid destroys the vessel which contains it. Which means much before you hurt the world with your anger you hurt yourself with your anger. Again I have to quote Buddha only, nobody put it better than him. He said 'there is no punishment for anger, you will be punished by your anger.'

TASK 5

Listen to the audio/video carefully and choose the most appropriate answer for the following questions.

1. According to the speaker, it is very easy to _____ the dog.

    A) Provoke   C) make angry

    B) bark on   D) irritate

2. The question of the speaker is not _____ are you but _____ are you?

    A) What, who   B) who, what   C) why, what   D) who, why

3. If you get angry, you become the _____ of the situation.

    A) Victim   B) slave   C) master   D) controller

4. "When you feel you are not in control of the situation, when nothing works you feel this will work." In this sentence "this" is used for_____

    A) Anger   B) patience   C) solution   D) your nature

5. When you get angry acids get _____ in your body.

    A) Mixed   B) bleeding   C) secreted   D) flowed

6. The speaker Quoted _____ in his speech.

    A) Vivekananda   B) Krishna   C) Rama   D) Buddha

7. Complete the Quotation "There is no _____ for anger; you will be _____ by your anger."

   A) one punished, punished   C) punishment, punished
   B) penalty, resulted   D) sentence, sentenced

Read the questions carefully and write down appropriate answer.

1. According the speaker what is the reason that one gets angry?

   _____
   _____
   _____
   _____
   _____

2. What is the first step suggested by the speaker to control your anger?

   _____
   _____
   _____
   _____
   _____

TRANSCRIPTION 6
WHAT IS THE THIRD EYE?

So what is referred to as a third eye is we always said, Shiva will open his third eye and he can burn up the whole existence if he wants. You need to understand this is a dialectical culture. You don't take these things literally logically. You need to always read behind it. Unfortunately people start interpreting it as a logical thing and it's whole thing is so badly distorted. Dimensions which cannot be expressed logically, they are always packed up in these kinds of stories so that they are persevered without distortion.

So Shiva opens his third eye and either everything burns up or he sees everything clearly. So third eye is not a physical thing it is just that if your energies reach a certain pick within you, you have a new clarity of vision of life. You see everything from a completely different dimension. So you start seeing things, it's an inner eye we say, we can say you can turn it inward or outward, whichever way you turn it. So these eyes are only outward, you can't roll your eye balls inwards and see what's within you, isn't it?

So third eye is both ways, if you want turn it inward or you can turn it outward. Whichever way you are seeing life beyond the normal limitations of your perception. Your perception has risen beyond the physical that is a third eye. Why is it connected to a particular spot in your body? Among the seven *Chakras,* the sixth dimension is called *Ajna*. Ajna is located slightly above where the eyebrows meet. There are three dimensions attached to it, these three dimensions are traditionally named after Shiva, three different forms of Shiva, but these three are actual experiential points in the body. Where if your energy moves to that point your experience of life alters itself. The whole process of whatever spiritual process you are doing consciously or unconsciously is fundamentally to move to a higher plane of perception, isn't it? yes?

You call it God, you call it *Kundalini*, you call it *yoga* you call it what you want but fundamentally the whole thing is to raise your perception from a limited physical perception to higher possibility. So if your energies are in lowest *chakra* which is referred to as the *Muldhara*, food and sleep will be the most dominating factors of your life, only food and sleep you will not know anything else. If energy moves to body Swadisthana than you are a pleasure seeker, you enjoy the physical world in so many different ways. If your energies move in Manipuraka then you are a doer in the world, you are an achiever. If you energy moves in to Anahata you are a creative person, may be you are an artist, you are a painter, you are something more creative about the life. If your energies move in to Visudhhi, you could become dominant there, you are a powerhouse. Power need not just mean this; human beings can be powerful in so many different ways. So this the power centre if energies move into your Ajna then you have clarity of vision. Now you are intellectually realised not experientially realised. Intellectually realised you touched a point where life can not disturb you, life cannot take a toll on you because intellectually you are realised but still you are not ecstatic. In any way you don't know the ecstasy of life but you have stability of life, nothing can touch you, nothing can disturb you, you come to that point. From the lowest point of Muldhara to Ajna there are many ways of reaching there. There are so many paths, a million different paths of how to get there. But from Ajna to Sahasra there is no way, it's a path less path. This is a reason why lot of people are talking only about peace because they only got till here and they don't know what's beyond. So they are assuming and concluding that's all that is. Because there is particular path or method to get beyond there are no particular methods or there are no methods. When all methods dropped only then from Ajna to Sahasra one will reach. If your energy touch your Sahasra, the top most chakra, you will become ecstatic like for no reason, simply you are ecstatic, you don't need any external stimulus. You will see those of you who come to the power spandana.

Simply ecstatic, nothing is happening. Nobody is telling you beautiful things, not any dinner-lottery, nothing. Simply you are ecstatic just blowing like that. Because your energies have hit the Sahasra. So from here to here there is no journey. So when you come here if you can turn this third eye inward, only then you see that there is no way, the only way is to jump. To jump into total emptiness either you must be crazy or you must have absolute trust in somebody else's word. There are only two ways you can jump into nothingness, isn't it? Either you must be crazy that you don't care what happens to you or you have so much trust in somebody, if he says jump you will anyway jump. There are only two ways. So the third eye is something that gives you a total clarity of how things are, how life processes. When I say life don't think of life waking up in the morning, eating, going to the party, not that life. Fundamental life, life as you, life as an entity, life as a basis of existence right now. When once you have a clear vision of this then the way you function, the way you conduct your life is very very different. So once your third eye opens it is not that this is going to split and open up, your perception has risen beyond the physical. You have started seeing that which is beyond the physical.

Question- Have you heard about those schools and they have blind so that they develop this ability to do remote healing?

Sadguru- No, those schools are fundamentally trying to develop the intuitive nature of the mind. But I am not talking about the mind when I say third eye. See mind is capable of fantastic things by itself. You have not explored even a small percentage of mind's capabilities. Human beings have not explored even a very small capabilities of the mind. What they are trying to do by closing off the eyes for a certain period is to develop an intuitive mind. See for example a person who is visually handicapped, his sense of the other four senses are very high, isn't it? have you noticed this? Their capability so uncanny about how they hear things, how they know things, just by the direction of the sound is so uncanny. So that is about heightening a certain aspect of the mind so that they become intuitive. That's a different dimension. If even in India people who want to trained in astrology, people who want to trained in predicting other people's life and things they shut their eyes off for long periods so that they learn to use their mind in a particular way. When I say third eye we are not talking about the mind at all. It doesn't involve the normal process of mind. It's a different dimension by itself.

TASK 6

Listen to the audio/video carefully and choose the most appropriate answer for the following questions.

1. Dimensions which cannot be expressed logically, they are always packed up in these kinds of _____ so they are _____ without distortion.

   A) Books, preserved   C) stories, sustained
   B) Stories, preserved   D) myths, sustained

2. There are _____ dimensions attached to Ajna and these dimensions are traditionally named after _____.

   A) Five, Shiva   C) four, Shiva
   B) three, Shiva   D) seven, Shiva

3. Match A with B. There are names of Chakras in A column and the factors related to the chakras in B column.

A		B
1. Muldhara	-	__-Ecstasy
2. Sahasra	-	__-Domination person, powerhouse
3. Manipuraka	-	__-Creative person, Artist, Painter
4. Swadistana	-	__-Food and sleep
5. Anahata	-	__-Pleasure seeker
6. Agna	-	__-Doer, achiever in the world
7. Visuddhi	-	__-Clarity of vision

4. **There are many ways, millions of ways to reach from the lowest point of Muldhara to Ajna but from Ajna to Sahasra there is/are_____ way(s).**

   A) one   B) many   C) two   D) no

5. **So if you want to reach Sahasra you need to jump into emptiness, and to jump into emptiness either you must be_____ or you must have absolute trust in somebody's _____.**

   A) lazy, world   B) crazy, world

   C) crazy, word   D) lazy, word

6. **Name the Chakras in their correct order.**

(Muldhara, Sahasra, Manipuraka, Swadistana, Anahata, Agna, Visuddhi)

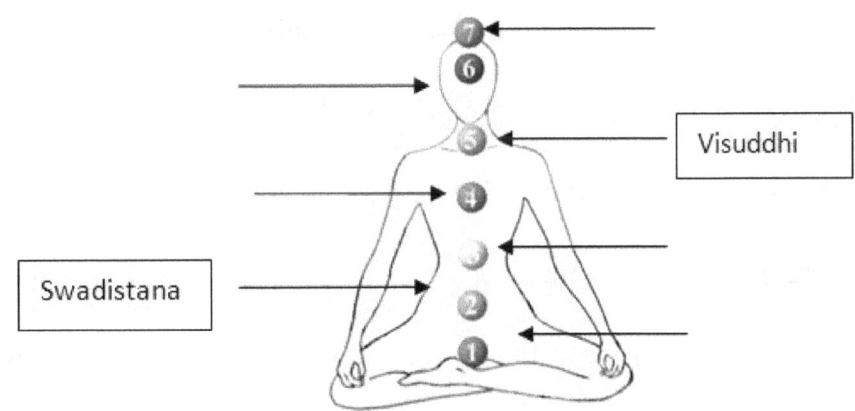

TRANSCRIPTION 7
WHAT ARE YOUR VIEWS ON TRAJECTORY OF INDIAN ENGLISH?

Question- What are your views on the trajectory of Indian English?

Answer- India is amazing. There are more people speaking English in India probably than in the rest of the mother tongue English speaking world combined. When I was last there, I asked everybody I met, how many people speak English in India now? And nobody knew. So people guessed all over the place and that consensus was that perhaps the third of the population speaks some sort of English. I am not saying to native speaker fluency level but certainly able to carry on a conversation of domestic subject matter. May be with all sorts of odd Indianisms here and there in case occasional errors and Standard English, whose standard English point of view and so on and obviously limitations in vocabulary and some of the most sophisticated grammatical construction not there and certainly sometimes with the very distinctive Indian accent. But nonetheless it is English. And that means that the figure must be three hundred million or four hundred million which is more than the combined population of Britain, Ireland, United States, Canada, Australia, New Zealand and South Africa. So something amazing is happening in India.

Now is Indian English changing as a consequence? Of course it is. You go to India and you will hear thousands of expressions that are local to India, not talking about things like 'Hinglish', which is a combination of Hindi and English, I am talking about features of Indian English generally used throughout the subcontinent. Different dialects of English even reflecting the different contact- situations with Hindi and Tamil and the other languages that are there. So there is a distinctive Indian English emerging mainly in vocabulary also in phonology, pronunciation and to some extent in grammar too. Is this going to impact on the world English as a whole? It all depends on the future of India. Language spreads because of power. If India becomes an increasingly powerful nation then Indian English will spread. Is it going to be powerful? It already is but specific in what specific ways well just look at the electronic revolution the way in which software and hardware and all the intellectual issues that surround the development of the internet are achieving, I think taking great strides in India. Where is the next Google going to come from people sometimes ask. I would not be surprised if it was India. And if what were the case then suddenly an Indian English which hitherto has been a rather dismissed variety of language will suddenly become rather sexy rather attractive. People will want to use it. They won't even consciously think about what wanting to, they will just start using it because some of the power brokers of the world are already using it. and then Indian English will come into its own.

TASK 7

Listen to the talk carefully and choose the most appropriate answer for the following questions.

1. There are more people speak English in India than the rest of _____ speaking world combined.

    A) English as a first language   C) English as a second language
    B) Mother tongue   D) native language

2. When David Crystal asked people how many people speak English in India? And people guessed and the consensus was_____

    A) Half of the population   C) half of the literate people
    B) Third of the literate   D) third of the population

3. Indians speak English with typical Indian accent and the figure of the people is 300 or 400 million which is more than combined population of_____, Ireland, _____, _____, Australia,_____ and South Africa.

    A) United States, Canada, Britain, New Zealand
    B) Britain, United States, Canada, New Zealand
    C) United States, New Zealand, Canada, Britain
    D) Canada, New Zealand, Ireland, United States.

4. When the speaker told if you go to India and you will hear thousands of expressions that are local to India, at that time he was not talking about _____.

    A) Indian English   B) English   C) Hinglish   D) Gujlish

5. **Language spreads because of _____.**

   A) Power   B) use   C) Internet   D) people

6. **What do people ask to David Crystal?**

   A) When is the next Google going to come?

   B) Where is the next Google going to be operated from?

   C) Where is the next Google going to come from?

   D) Where is the next Google going to come to?

7. **According to speaker what is the future of Indian English?**

   A) It will be difficult to use it with the world

   B) It will be used all over the world

   C) It will vanish

   D) It is difficult to say, not sure

TRANSCRIPTION 8
FACE WHAT YOU MUST FACE

I am just reminded of a small story and an episode from The Mahabharata. Where Krishna and Balrama going to the forest and by then the Sun had already set and it was dark and it was a time when we did not have forest resorts for people to stay so it seems Krishna came up with a proposal to Balrama, "I will go to sleep and you keep watching me. Whenever you feel sleepy you wake me up and I will keep watching and you can go to sleep" and Krishna went to sleep. Balrama who kept loitering to and fro, encountered a monster in the forest and the monster screamed at the Balrama and Balrama who was shaken up by the monster, shrank in size and the monster became bigger than Balrama. The monster screamed one more time, Balrama shrank even further and the monster became even bigger. One last attempt the monster screamed at Balrama, unable to take the mind of the monster Balrama screamed 'Krishna' and he fainted. Hearing the call 'Krishna', Krishna woke up though Balrama had fainted he mistook Balrama to be sleeping and Krishna started walking to and fro. So the monster which had seen now a new person standing there, screamed at the one more time. And it seems Krishna instead of being perturbed stared at the monster and asked "what do you want?" The courage of Krishna made Krishna expand and the monster shrunk. The monster once again screamed at Krishna, Krishna again asked the monster "what do you want?" the monster shrank even further and Krishna expanded even more. One last attempt the monster screamed at Krishna and Krishna again asked the monster "what do you want?" And the monster shrank in size. The epic goes Krishna takes that monster and ties and knot at the end of his dhoti and places the monster inside. The Sun did rise and Balrama and Krishna began to walk and as they were walking it seems Balrama told Krishna "you don't know what happened last night, a monster came and it was threatening us so much" Krishna gently took the monster out of his dhoti and showed to Balrama and asked, "are you talking about this?" Immediately Balrama says "But when I saw it was so big how come it had become so small?"

And Veda Vyas trough the voice of Krishna says "when you avoid what you must face in life it becomes bigger than you and takes control over you. When you face what you must face you become bigger than it and you take control over it" The monster here the Veda Vyas is referring to is all the challenges that we face in life and Veda Vyas want you and me to realize through the voice of Krishna, "if you keep avoiding what you must face, these challenges become monstrous and they gain control over you, instead face what you must face and you become larger than it and you gain control over it" so when you realize the very challenges of life, the very experiences of life, the very tough times of life, are not there, the

Furnace is not there to burn you but to transform you in to a glittering silver, very purpose of experiences of life is to make you what you can be. So from now onwards whenever you face anything in life, always remember it has been given to you for purpose for you to become what you can become.

TASK 8

Listen to the audio/video and choose the most appropriate option.

1. **Which of the following two characters are mentioned in the narrative?**

    A) Krishna and Arjuna   C) Krishna and Sahdev

    B) Krishna and Balrama   D) Krishna and Bheem

2. **According to the speaker the forest did not have the facility of_____**

    A) Ashrams   B) Taverns   C) Resorts   D) Inns

3. **What duty did Krishna assign to his companion before he went to sleep**

    A) To loiter to and from   B) To loiter to and fro

    C) To loiter from place to place   D) To loiter across the forest

4. **What happened when monster screamed last time at Krishna's companion?**

    A) he became bigger than monster

    B) Monster became bigger than him

    C) he fainted

    D) Krishna came to his rescue

5. **On seeing his companion lying down on the ground Krishana thought he(companion) was _____**

    A) fooling the monster   C) fooling him(Krishna)

    B) Ridiculing the monster   D) sleeping fast

6. When monster screamed at Krishna first time, instead of being perturbed Krishna asked him_____
   A) Who he was
   B) What he was
   C) What he wanted
   D) What was his problem

7. The term 'perturbed' in the above mentioned sentence means_____
   A) To be worried   B) to be angry
   C) To be scared   D) to be shocked

   Read the questions carefully and write down appropriate answer.

8. What did Krishna do to the monster when monster turned in to smallest size?
   _____
   _____
   _____
   _____

9. According to the speaker through the voice of Krishna what is the message of Veda Vyasa?
   _____
   _____
   _____
   _____
   _____

10. What was the Krishna's proposal to his companion?
_____
_____
_____
_____
_____

TRANSCRIPTION 9

Interviewer	:	hi mam, thank you for joining us.
Shobbha De	:	my pleasure
Interviewer	:	mam, you visited to a number book festivals in the past from London to Mumbai and now Sarjaha, so what do you think these books festivals are able to achieve.
Shobbha De	:	Well one the encouraging part of any lit fest is that authors get to meet the readers. To me that is the single most important thing. Because otherwise writing is the lonely profession, you write in isolation, your book is out there, gets published and you don't always know who your reader is. But I have seen the enthusiasm with which not the publishers participate but the numbers of readers who have turned up and for them to interact with an author who is by line they familiar with but they have never really had the opportunity to ask the person why did you write this or what is the meaning behind that or what about this book or what you are writing next. It's a kind of

		personal interface that's very important to the readers as well as to the authors. And from the trade point of view a lit fests get-together publishers from sometimes across the world and it's a great opportunity for publishers and authors to interact and for the rights to be sold in other countries and other languages. So as a trade activity it's very very key.
Interviewer	:	we're now living in an era where the world is getting more and more digitalize so what do you think is the relevance of paperback books in the world of digital era.
Shobbha de	:	well, I see books coexisting quite comfortably is like when television became very big, and the television news became the hottest medium people thought the news paper would die out but it hasn't. So people have a choice today they can watch television, they can watch the news, they can read the news, they can read analysis, they can comment in a news paper, which they don't always get on television. So similarly the physical book I think for a lot of readers will continue to be, may be a preferred book. But a younger

	generation is going to switch to digitalized books but still I feel that the...the....the.... kind of sensual experience that you derive from holding a book, turning its pages, even just the smell and even aging of a book is something that can't be easily weaken.
Interviewer	: being aware in opinion it is almost prerequisite in today's era of information overload. As an individualistic person yourself do you believe in this quality as an act of asset for a person?
Sobbhha de	: well, you know to be able to express an opinion there has to be something behind that opinion, it can't be a random opinion. You have to have some authority, you have to have some experience, you got to have an informed comment to make on any situation, all, and you have to have credibility you can't just keep shooting your mouth of on anything and everything. And no one is going to listen so for those people who call themselves or was perceived as opinion shapers or opinion maker, it's because their opinions count. And people look out for that opinion because it also gives them perspectives. So if it's wonderful to be able

		express your opinion freely and in a democracy we should take advantage of that, that's what the blogosphere is there for. And tweeter of course it's an all out war on tweeter which is fabulous, it's fantastic, it's very democratic. The more opinion you have as a young person the better it is but it should always be a backed by knowledge and also opinion carries responsibilities as well.
Interviewer	:	in this region particularly of lit a number of students inspired to be a writer so as a writer yourself and an accomplished one of that what would you like to tell the students to do?
Shobbha de	:	well you know, yahh for young writers the most important thing to retain is originality. So you must not try and write like someone else, you have to find out your own voice. And as a publisher myself that's what I for when I get manuscripts from young writers and I get a lot of them, I get may be ten a week but you can always tell a writer who is trying to aim a senior writer and the writer who really has the confidence to say what he or she wants to say in their

own unique way. So I would say the more you write the better you get at it. It's a little like classical music like doing riyas, if you do it every morning your voice is that much more supple, if you write every day of your life even if the five hundred words , your writing becomes more supple and just gets better.

Interviewer : And finally mam you have written for number of columns in news papers, magazines even penned TV show, gone on to become an anchor and then an author, so what's next to Shobbha De?

Shobbha De : well, I have a new book coming up next year. I have gone back to fiction after 13 years so it's a huge challenge; I have been doing non-fiction all this while. And wring fiction in a way librates you and its fantastic very freeing, wonderful feeling. As so I am looking forward to that and I am looking forward to the first of my books from my own imprint which is the Shobbha De book which I am doing for Penguin. So which means again working with new voices, working with new authors and coming up with books I hope it will appeal to a wide readership.

Interviewer   :   it was a pleasure having you with us here. Thank you

TASK 9

Listen to the talk carefully and choose the most appropriate answer for the following questions.

1. Where did the current interview take place?

   A) Mumbai   B) Australia   C) Sarjah   D) London

2. What is the encouraging part and the single most important thing about the lit festivals for Shobbha De?

   A) Authors get to meet readers
   B) Authors get to meet other authors
   C) Readers get the diverse literature
   D) One can get the literature at low prise

3. The interviewer asked Shobbha De about the importance of _____ books in the era of digitalization.

   A) Paperpack   C) digital
   B) paperback   D) E (e-books)

4. When television became very big and the television news became the hottest medium people thought the news paper would _____ but it hasn't.

   A) Pass away   C) Die away
   B) Die out   D) pass out

49

5. The sensual experience which you derive from holding a copy book, turning its pages even just the _____ and even _____ of a book is something that can't be easily weakened.
   A) Smell, aging   C) smell, edging
   B) small, Aging   D) small, edging

6. People look for good and neutral opinions as they give them_____.
   A) Knowledge   C) information
   B) perspective   D) thought

7. The interviewee said that 'it is good to share more opinions being younger but it should be backed by_____.
   A) Information   B) responsibility   C) knowledge   D) person

8. Shobbha De said: for young writers it is very important to _____ the originality, they must not try to write like someone else.
   A) Retain   B) copy   C) follow   D) regain

9. If you write every day of your life even if the five hundred words, your writing becomes more _____ and just gets better.
   A) Subtle   B) Supple   C) concrete   D) original

10. Shobbha De was writing non-fiction for 13 years and she is moving towards fiction so she said that writing fiction _____you and its fantastic very freeing, wonderful feeling.
    A) Constrains   B) makes creative   C) liberates   D) bounds

TRANSCRIPTION 10

Interviewer : Here is now tradition to introduce Nassaruddin Shah as India's finest actor. So traditional infact that I suspect his rather bored of that description. So I am not going to call him India's finest actor though of course he is, but I am going to focus on something else on how innovative he is being, he started out with art cinema moved to commercial cinema, he has done television, he anchored cricket shows and he has done theatre. Many many things, many many different things.

Naseeruddin Shah : I guess that is what makes life worthwhile <u>live</u>. You going to try everything that you feel, you shouldn't an attempt to grab at every dream you ever had. So I have had dreams earliest once of being an actor, I also had dreams of being a cricketer, I had also dreams of being a film maker, I always wanted to be on the stage. So I consider myself pretty blessed that I have had the opportunity to try my hand at all these things.

Interviewer	:	anything you wanted to do you haven't done so far?
Naseeruddin Shah	:	ya I really really want to make a film.....
Interviewer	:	what kind of film is it, without giving too much away....
Naseeruddin Shah	:	to put into one sentence, a kind of film that I would like to see. I am not fond of hindi commercial cinema, I never was. I always consider these films rather silly and they never caught my fancy. I was fascinated by the Eling studio's comedies when I was a child and I loved westerns always, I loved war movies, through my childhood I was exposed to films like 'Waterfront', 'citizen gained' and all the old ranged, 'Zoro rides again' and 'Mickey mouse', so movies turned me on from the very early age and so did cricket. These two passions went side by side.
Interviewer	:	I don't know whether it is deliberate, you haven't mentioned any Hindi movies....

Naseeruddin Shah : well, firstly we never saw any Hindi Movies in school. Secondly my dad was rather particular about what movies we saw when we went home. And so he would accompany us to see these movies. So we saw them under a strict supervision. And so I never really had any heroes in the hindi film world I must admit. Do there were actors I liked, people liked Motilal and Balraj Sani and Yakub but I can't say any of the actors of hindi cinema inspired me greatly.

Interviewer : None of the directors? Because now it is traditional and our board starts coming in saying Raj Kapoor, Guru Gutt, this is what I want to do but…

Naseeruddin Shah : no I discovered Guru Dutt and vimal Roy's movies much later.

Interviewer : Ok, so they weren't formative influence…

Naseeruddin Shah : no they were not. People who were formative influences on me were actors like Anthony Quinn, Paul Muni, Spencer Tracy, Charles Lotan, these kind of people. Not the Cluck Gabbles….

Interviewer : That is what I said, not the heroes…

Naseeruddin Shah : not the heroes because I didn't identify with those guys. I thought these are not real human beings, these are photographic tricks.

Interviewer : Paul Muni is more of less forgotten but Dilip Kumar who I once interviewed cited as his role model as well.

Naseeruddin Shah : Paul Muni was perhaps the first actor who made it a business of playing believable characters. As he was famous for the quality of him makeup and the quality of the physical attitudes that he took or…

Interviewer : It became the character

Naseeruddin Shah : became the character and also played a large number of historical characters.

Interviewer : Were you fascinated by the people who played historical characters?

Naseeruddin Shah : it hasn't struck me that way but the fact that they were able to recreate characters whose pictures we saw in history books…

Interviewer : And make them come alive…

Naseeruddin Shah	:	…and make them come alive. That was totally fascinating. Quinn and Tracy fascinated me for another reason because they were blugg ugliest kinds of things you know. They were not hot throbs.
Interviewer	:	Did you feel ever that you are not good looking enough to become an actor?
Naseeruddin Shah	:	yes, not only that. I didn't feel that I was either that tall or that well built or that magnetic as people like John Wayne and Gary Cooper and so on. And so I never bothered, to aspired to that kind of thing.
Interviewer	:	you not really instant commercial cinema, you feel you are not good looking enough to become a leading man, so what keeps you going?
Naseeruddin Shah	:	I think it was the desire to be other people. I was an unhappy kid, I had no friends, I was not popular in school, I wasn't good at anything.
Interviewer	:	were you like a jerk as something or….
Naseeruddin Shah	:	I was one of those wall flowers who nobody notices and nobody pays any attention to. And I

		think that the teachers in that school made it their job to systematically destroy whatever little confidence I had. Because I was not good at studies, I wasn't good at games,
Interviewer	:	Were you sort of introverted?
Naseeruddin Shah	:	yes, I was withdrawn, I didn't speak much not because I had nothing to say but because I thought I'd make a fool of myself the moment I'll open my mouth.
Interviewer	:	So it was confidence.
Naseeruddin Shah	:	it was a question of confidence and I resent very much the fact that those teachers never bothered to delve a little deeper into what I was all about and find out the how come a child who stands first in English composition and English text fails in English grammar.
Interviewer	:	Something clearly wrong.
Naseeruddin Shah	:	and no one ever bothered. Of course I got zero in Maths and physics and chemistry just went totally over my head.

Interviewer	:	The other problem not having confidence is that actor requires a degree of unselfconsciousness a degree of confidence? How did you bridge that?
Naseeruddin Shah	:	I think that the most people who go into acting because it is a passion, are people who been unhappy, children who felt incomplete, as children and who despise themselves as children.
Interviewer	:	You really despise yourself …?
Naseeruddin Shah	:	ya, ya
Interviewer	:	How did you feel, what did you feel?
Naseeruddin Shah	:	I was convinced that I was foolish and that I was incapable of understanding complicated things like mathematics and physics which my other classmates…
Interviewer	:	All knew easily…
Naseeruddin Shah	:	All knew easily.
Interviewer	:	And why didn't you make friends?
Naseeruddin Shah	:	I was scared. I still hesitate to approach people whom I don't know, I am pretty terrified meeting strangers. When I am on a flight I invariably shut

		my eyes and go to sleep or pretend to be asleep so that the guy sitting next to me won't strike up a conversation.
Interviewer	:	I know you feel…
Naseeruddin Shah	:	so I am deeply grateful that I could find my vocation and I could not dare confess this deep desire to anybody except my two brothers who were extremely supportive but I dare not to confess to my dad who would have probably beating the hell out of me if I say…
Interviewer	:	so what did you say when you left the school? What did you say you are going to do?
Naseeruddin Shah	:	well as luck would have it I failed in class 9.
Interviewer	:	You failed?
Naseeruddin Shah	:	I got zero in trigonometry, I got five out of hundred in physics…
Interviewer	:	Just the science subjects…
Naseeruddin Shah	:	ya and so on. So my dad pulled me out of this place which he said was too expensive for an idiot like me and he put me into a school where he

thought he can keep an eye on me. And as fate would have it in this school which was run by Indian Jesuit priests in Ajmer, a school called St. Anselm's. I got together a group of friends and we did a selections, scenes from The Merchant of Venice in which I played Shylock, in which I did a close imitation of my all time favorite Jeffery Campbell and suddenly my whole life changed.

Interviewer : Just because u went to a less prestigious school.

Naseeruddin Shah : ya, went to a less prestigious school.

TASK 10

Listen to the talk carefully and choose the most appropriate answer for the following questions.

1) What kind of film does Nasaruddin Shah want to make?

   A. A film that his audience would like to see

   B. A film that he would like to see

   C. A film that appeals to audience

   D. A film that relates with real life

2) What kind of films does Nasaruddin not like?

   A) He did not like art movies

   B) He did not like commercial movies

   C) He did not like suspense movies

   D) He did not like action movies

3) Which of the two passions does he talk about?

   A) Cricket and studies

   B) Cricket and photography

   C) Acting and cricket

   D) Acting and reading

4) What kind of kid was he?

   A) nervous

   B) extrovert

   C) alienated

   D) diffident

5) In which area of English paper did he not do well?

A) English composition B) English text

C) English grammar D) English criticism

6) What do you understand by the expression "strike up conversation"?

A) To start a conversation

B) To conclude a conversation

C) To change the topic of conversation

D) To comment on the conversation

7) Which members supported Nasaruddin in his passion?

A) Parents C) Sisters

B) Grandparents D) brothers

8) What does he say about his performance in science subjects?

A) He was good

B) He did not do well

C) He was average

D) He was brilliant

9) What does he say about teachers in the first school?

_____
_____
_____
_____

10) What was the turning point in Nasaruddin's life?

_____
_____
_____
_____

References

David Crystal. (2010 , January 20). David Crystal -How is the internet changing language today?[Video file].Retrieved from https://www.youtube.com/watch?v=P2XVdDSJHqY.

David Crystal. (2010 , July 27). David Crystal - What are your views on the trajectory of Indian English? [Video file]. Retrieved from https://www.youtube.com/watch?v=zhaaGjUPxd4.

Mahatria Ra. (2012 , December 4). Mahatria...How to deal with anger...Daily Messages[Video file]. Retrieved from https://www.youtube.com/watch?v=Gs1nCVMNEeU.

Mahatria Ra. (2012 , December 4). Mahatria...How to deal with anger...Daily Messages[Video file]. Retrieved from https://www.youtube.com/watch?v=Gs1nCVMNEeU.

Mahatria Ra. (2013 , July 15). A Mom at School by Mahatria- (infinitheism)- Inspiring talk on teachers [Video file]. Retrieved from https://www.youtube.com/watch?v=d63O8Gnadns.

Mahatria Ra. (2013 , July 19). Face what you must Face by Mahatria - infinitheism (motivational, inspirational talk)[Video file]. Retrieved from https://www.youtube.com/watch?v=S729dQ_9WXA.

Mahatria Ra. (2013 , October 8). Mahatria Laughter in Families - By Mahatria (infinitheism) - motivational talk [Video file]. Retrieved from https://www.youtube.com/watch?v=hcfj5h_bGWI.

Naseeruddin Shah. (2012 , July 3). Naseeruddin Shah - Cover Story - Very Innovative Interview - HD[Video file]. Retrieved from https://www.youtube.com/watch?v=JZIc4U87Mr4.

Sadguru. (2010 , May 2010) What is the Third Eye? Sadhguru [Video file]. Retrieved from https://www.youtube.com/watch?v=VTeKP4g0a4k.

Sadguru. (2012 , March 19). A Truth about Being happy -- Sadguru...[Video file].Retrieved from. https://www.youtube.com/watch?v=Eg8GJGw8i90.

Shobhaa De. (2011 , November 22). Interview with Shobhaa De[Video file]. Retrieved from https://www.youtube.com/watch?v=mqTelDJsJQE.

www.ingramcontent.com/pod-product-compliance
Lightning Source LLC
Chambersburg PA
CBHW081136170426
43197CB00017B/2883